SPIDERS SET I

TARANTULA SPIDERS

Tamara L. Britton
ABDO Publishing Company

visit us at
www.abdopublishing.com

Published by ABDO Publishing Company, 8000 West 78th Street, Edina, Minnesota 55439. Copyright © 2011 by Abdo Consulting Group, Inc. International copyrights reserved in all countries. No part of this book may be reproduced in any form without written permission from the publisher. The Checkerboard Library™ is a trademark and logo of ABDO Publishing Company.

Printed in the United States of America, North Mankato, Minnesota.
042010
092010

 PRINTED ON RECYCLED PAPER

Cover Photo: iStockphoto
Interior Photos: AP Images p. 7; iStockphoto pp. 5, 9, 11, 12, 15, 19;
    Peter Arnold pp. 17, 21; Thinkstock p. 16

Editor: BreAnn Rumsch
Art Direction & Cover Design: Neil Klinepier

Library of Congress Cataloging-in-Publication Data

Britton, Tamara L., 1963-
  Tarantula spiders / Tamara L. Britton.
     p. cm. -- (Spiders)
  Includes bibliographical references and index.
  ISBN 978-1-61613-442-6
  1. Tarantulas--Juvenile literature. I. Title.
  QL458.42.T5B75 2011
  595.4'4--dc22
                      2010009629

Contents

TARANTULA SPIDERS

Spiders are arachnids. They have two body parts and eight legs. All arachnids are arthropods. So, their skeletons are on the outside of their bodies. Spiders are also ectothermic. This means they get their body heat from their surroundings.

Scientists recognize 109 spider families. Within these families there are 38,000 species. That's a lot of spiders! About 800 of these species are in the family **Theraphosidae**.

Throughout the world, people call large members of this family by different names. They are called baboon spiders in Africa. In South

America, Australia, New Guinea, and Asia they are called bird-eating spiders. In North America, these huge spiders are known as tarantulas.

The tarantula is named after an Italian wolf spider. Victims of its bite were said to wildly dance about!

SIZES

Many people believe tarantulas are huge, hairy spiders. They certainly are hairy! But some are actually quite small.

Some pinktoe tarantulas have a body length of less than 1.5 inches (4 cm). Their leg span is about 5 inches (13 cm) across. The world's tiniest tarantula lives in Belize. Its leg span is just 2 inches (5 cm)!

Still, some tarantulas are indeed big. The African king baboon spider's body can be more than 3 inches (7.5 cm) long. Its leg span measures almost 10 inches (25 cm) across.

North American species are just a bit smaller. The colorful Mexican redknee tarantula can have a leg span of more than 5 inches (13 cm).

Some tarantulas are popular as pets!

The biggest spider in the world is a tarantula! The goliath birdeater has a body length of 3 inches (7.5 cm). Yet, its leg span is an amazing 11 inches (28 cm) across. That's a big spider!

SHAPES

Tarantulas are often recognized for their thick, hairy bodies. Their two body sections are almost round in shape. The front body part is called the **cephalothorax**. It is protected by a plate called the carapace. The rear body part is called the **abdomen**.

The cephalothorax contains the spider's brain, **venom** glands, and stomach. Six pairs of **appendages** also connect to it. At the front of the cephalothorax are two **chelicerae**. Each is tipped with a fang. Next to them are two **pedipalps**.

Finally, four pairs of legs line the spider's sides. Each leg ends with claws that help the spider grip surfaces.

A slim waist connects the cephalothorax and the abdomen. It is called the pedicel. The spider's

Spider Anatomy

ABDOMEN

SPINNERETS

PEDICEL

CEPHALOTHORAX

CHELICERA

PEDIPLAP

CARAPACE

LEG

intestines, nerve cord, and blood vessels all pass through it.

The **abdomen** hold's the spider's heart. It is also where the lungs, **digestive** tract, reproductive and respiratory **organs**, and silk glands are located. The silk glands make the tarantula's silk. Spinnerets on the end of the abdomen spin the silk from the spider's body.

COLORS

Many tarantulas have black or brown bodies. Yet some are still very colorful. The Chilean rose tarantula has a brown body. But, its rose-colored hairs make it appear pink. The Mexican redknee tarantula's body is also brown. But, bright orange highlights its legs and **cephalothorax**.

The tiger rump tarantula from Costa Rica has a black body. A reddish cephalothorax and stripes on its **abdomen** look tigerlike! Asian species, such the ornamental rain forest tarantula, can have wildly patterned bodies and legs.

Some tarantulas are brilliantly colored. The greenbottle blue tarantula has blue legs, a green

The beautiful, gentle Mexican redknee became such a popular pet that its population became threatened. So today, exporting it from Mexico is illegal.

carapace, and an orange **abdomen**! The African orange baboon spider is bright yellow. It has a sunburst marking on its carapace.

WHERE THEY LIVE

Tarantulas live on every continent except Antarctica. Most live along the **equator**. This area includes everything from tropical to dry regions.

Tarantulas are found in many different kinds of **habitats**. The Mexican blond tarantula lives in dry desert scrublands in the United States and Mexico. Other species, such as the East African horned baboon spider, live in African rain forests.

Tarantulas do not spin webs to live in. They line

Central and South American species, such as the greenbottle blue tarantula, like moist surroundings.

Where Do Tarantula Spiders Live?

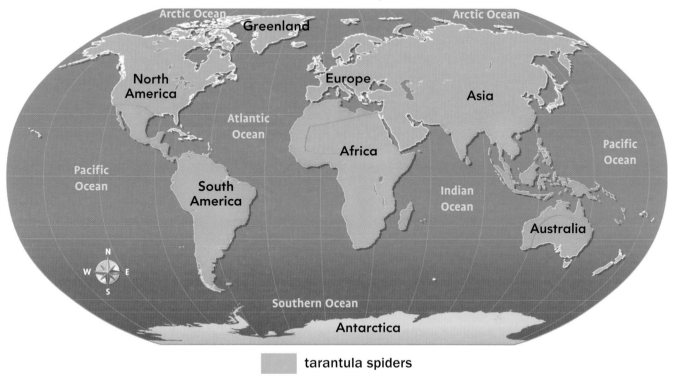

tarantula spiders

their nests with silk. Some species nest in burrows. They use their **chelicerae**, fangs, and **pedipalps** to dig the burrows. Others live in trees, where they make silken tubes in which to hide. Ground-dwelling species live under leaves or rocks.

SENSES

Tarantulas have eight eyes. That's a lot of eyes! Yet even with all those eyes, tarantulas cannot see very well. Since most species are active at night, their eyes mainly detect light levels. So, tarantulas must rely on other senses to survive in their surroundings.

The hairs on a tarantula's legs and **pedipalps** are sensitive to vibrations. They help the spider feel its way along its path. The hairs can also sense when something is nearby. This helps the spider to hunt prey.

Hollow hairs at the ends of their pedipalps and legs give tarantulas the senses of taste and smell. Now you know why tarantulas have such hairy bodies!

The pinktoe tarantula's hairs help it move around, find food, taste, smell, and defend itself.

DEFENSE

Tarantulas have many enemies. Mammals, birds, reptiles, and **amphibians** like to eat them. Humans capture the spiders to sell as pets.

Many tarantulas use camouflage to defend themselves against enemies. Even brightly colored species can be difficult to see in their **habitats**.

Some tarantulas use stridulation to scare off attackers. They rub their legs together to make a loud hissing sound.

Tarantulas in North and South America can defend

The tarantula hawk wasp lays its eggs inside live tarantulas. When the eggs hatch, the baby wasps eat the tarantula alive!

Orange baboon spiders are fast and aggressive. They will not hesitate to defend themselves.

themselves by flinging special hairs at their attacker. These urticating hairs are located on the spider's **abdomen**. They are very irritating to the skin of a human or a predator. It is painful for a predator if the hairs get into its eyes.

If these defenses do not work, the tarantula may rear back and show its fangs. This defensive posture tells enemies the tarantula will bite! While the bite isn't usually dangerous to humans, it can be painful.

FOOD

Tarantulas are carnivores. These hungry spiders will eat any animal they can overpower. This includes insects, other spiders, frogs, lizards, snakes, mice, and birds.

When a tarantula gets hungry, it leaves its shelter. It hides nearby and waits for prey. When prey approaches, the spider pounces!

The tarantula grabs its prey with its **pedipalps** and bites with its fangs. The spider's **venom** **paralyzes** the victim.

Then, the spider crushes its prey with its **chelicerae** and pours **digestive** juices on it. The juices turn the prey to liquid, which the tarantula sucks up!

A tarantula will continue to bathe its prey in digestive juices until it has eaten the entire meal.

BABIES

To preserve their population, tarantulas must reproduce. Tarantulas mate once a year. To mate, a male approaches a female. He drums his legs or moves his body in a special way. This way, the female knows he is not prey!

The female lays eggs during the summer. When she is ready, the female spins a silken pad. She lays 100 to 1,000 eggs on it. She then spins an egg sac around the eggs and guards it.

Depending on their species, the baby spiders hatch in two weeks to three months. Baby spiders are called spiderlings. After hatching, the spiderlings often stay near their mother. But soon, they go their own way.

As they grow, the spiderlings **shed** their **exoskeletons**. This is called molting. As adults, the spiders will still molt on occasion.

After about three years, the spiders are mature. Male tarantulas do not live long after reaching maturity. Females can live about 25 years.

Some pinktoe tarantula spiderlings are blue!

GLOSSARY

abdomen - the rear body section of an arthropod, such as an insect or a spider.

amphibian - an animal that can live in water and on land. Frogs, toads, and salamanders are amphibians.

appendage - a smaller body part that extends from the main body of a plant or an animal.

cephalothorax (seh-fuh-luh-THAWR-aks) - the front body section of an arachnid that includes the head and the thorax.

chelicera (kih-LIH-suh-ruh) - either of the front, leglike organs of an arachnid that has a fang attached to it.

digestive - of or relating to the breakdown of food into simpler substances the body can absorb.

equator - an imaginary circle around the middle of Earth. It is halfway between the North and South poles.

exoskeleton - the outer covering or structure that protects an animal, such as an insect.

habitat - a place where a living thing is naturally found.

organ - a part of an animal or a plant composed of several kinds of tissues. An organ performs a specific function. The heart, liver, gallbladder, and intestines are organs of an animal.